THE STRANGE CASE OF THE END OF CIVILISATION AS WE KNOW IT...

Few people know that when the legendary Sherlock Holmes ended his life, the Holmes family tree continued and produced, in time, a grandson named Arthur. The stories of Holmes and his trusted colleague, Dr Watson, were passed on from father to son and grandson, and such was the esteem in which Arthur held his grandfather's profession that he honoured his roots by taking rooms in Baker Street with a direct descendant of Dr Watson, by the name of William. Many of the family attributes were passed down, if somewhat warped by time and scientific progress (William Watson's physique, for example, had benefited by the acquisition of various bionic parts).

It was not until quite recently that Arthur, William and the world at large found out that Sherlock Holmes's arch-enemy Moriarty had also spawned some characteristic offspring. It is the inter action of these characters which has produced the present threat of THE END OF CIVILISATION AS WE KNOW IT

3

John Cleese, Jack Hobbs and Joe McGrath

The strange case of the end of civilisation as we know it

A Star book published by the paperback division of
W H ALLEN & Co. Ltd.

A Star Book
Published in 1977
by the Paperback Division of
W.H. Allen & Co. Ltd
A Howard and Wyndham Company
44 Hill Street, London, W.1.

Designed by Lawrence Edwards
Illustrations by George Djurkovic

Copyright© 1977 by Shearwater Productions

Typesetting by Yale Press Ltd., London SE25

Printed in Great Britain by
Hunt Barnard, Webb Offset Ltd. Aylesbury, Bucks.

ISBN   0 351 30109 0

SCENE 1

WELCOME DR. GROPINGER!

HAVE A NICE STAY HENRY!

Thus a happy placard-carrying crowd of Arabs welcome the famous Henry Gropinger as his plane swings down on T.E. Lawrence Airport. Dignitaries and Arab troops, backed by the characteristic melodies of a military band, line the runway.

INSIDE THE PLANE. . .

International Peacemaker Henry Gropinger is transfixed by an in-flight movie when suddenly, at the click of a switch, the movie soundtrack grinds to a halt. A voice coughs over the intercom:

> Excuse me, Mr. Secretary sir, this is the Captain speaking, we are about to land. I'm sorry but I have to ask you to fasten your sea belt, sir. Personally speaking, I hope you enjoyed your flight.

GROPINGER
— pointing to the film screen and whining like a child whose sweets have been taken away —

> Miss Goodbody just what exactly's happening here?

HOSTESS

> Dr. Gropinger?

GROPINGER

> Here!

— gesticulating at the screen —

> I am desirous of seeing the denouement of the motion picture. DOES HE GET THE GIRL?

HOSTESS

> Yes, but only a leg and a breast. Their plane crashes and they eat each other. Sir, would you *please* fasten your seatbelt?

She moves on up the aisle.

GROPINGER
— *calling after her* —

Eh Miss! Can you come back here a minute?

— *she moves in; he sips his drink* —

I need to know what day it is. Let's see. . .Monday was
Northern Ireland, Tuesday uh. . .Rhodesia. . .

—*Gropinger feels in his pockets for his diary* —

. . .Where's my diary! I had it on me when we took off.
It has to be here somewhere. Gentlemen. . .my diary, I need
my diary. Find it!

*Henry Gropinger's staff of CIA Men, Secretaries, Call Girls etc., search the
plane and each other for Gropinger's personal diary. Shoulder holsters and
shoulder straps are busily adjusted. The CIA Men lean against the wall in the
classic "Assume the Position" manner (arms and legs outstretched) as they
search each other vainly.*

*In the background, behind the seaching group, one Francine Moriarty,
dressed as a Uniformed Steward, pockets a diary.*
Finally, an American Air Hostess addresses the searching executives:

Gentlemen, we're about to land. Dr. Gropinger, sir, would
you *please* sit down and fasten your seat belt?

The group obey her reluctantly.

GROPINGER
— seating himself and buckling his belt —

> Okay, Miss, but I need my diary. I don't know *where* I am
> or *who* I'm supposed to be meeting next! I'm suffering
> from a jet lag situation.

He peers out of the plane's window at the fast approaching ground.

*Meanwhile at T.E. Lawrence Airport, the military band continues to play as
the steps are pushed up against the plane. The doors open and Two Stern
American Marines appear flanking the door. The smiling Gropinger waves; the
crowd cheers; the Arabic Soldiers present arms; the Dignitaries smile.
The band finishes playing and there is silence.
Gropinger clears his throat and for a moment seems uncertain but in a voice
heard by everybody on the tarmac he gives his greeting to the welcoming
committee:*

> Lochaim!

— He pauses, less confidently. Testingly, he ventures —

> Muzzeltof?

*The smiles freeze. Gropinger looks worried. The Arabic Guard of Honour
level their rifles and as one man, on a command, shoot him down where he
stands. There is a smattering of applause from the Arab crowd. The conductor
gets attention and the orchestra starts to play once more.*

SCENE 2

THE MALL, LONDON...

Arthur Sherlock Holmes and Dr. Watson take their morning constitutional cycling on a tandem around the Victoria monument in front of Buckingham Palace, blissfully unaware of the momentous happenings which will soon bring them employment.

SCENE 3

MEANWHILE IN AMERICA AT THE WHITE HOUSE ITSELF...

A Black CIA Man picks up a bleeping 'phone, gulps and speaks:

White House here.

PRESIDENT

Tell him I'm out.

BLACK CIA MAN

No, no this is the White House...
No, the Chinese Take-Away is 21664.
This is 21164. That's O.K., we get a lot of their
calls.

The Black CIA Man replaces the receiver. The President, an accident prone, genial bull of a man, is seated behind his desk under a painting of Abraham Lincoln. The Stars and Stripes are in evidence too. He gets to his feet knocking over a glass of water and his chair. Brushing the water from his trousers, the President speaks:

Just a minute, now just a minute. Are you guys
telling me Gropinger didn't know which country
he was in?

FIRST CIA MAN (KLEIN)

Affirmative, sir. At that moment in time he was
suffering from a jet lag situation.

PRESIDENT

And as of now he's suffering from a death
situation. That's as of now, of course. Right?

13

FIRST CIA MAN

You just said as of now, sir.

PRESIDENT

What?

FIRST CIA MAN

I just said you just said as of now twice sir,
already.

PRESIDENT

Don't call me, sir. I'm the President. Now tell me
again, saying Mr. President at the end of the
sentence.

— He makes a sweeping gesture and knocks over a flag —

FIRST CIA MAN

I only said you just already said as of now twice
already, Mr. President.

PRESIDENT

Don't tell me what I just said.

FIRST CIA MAN

But you told me to tell you what I just said.

PRESIDENT

Don't tell me what I just told you to say.

— The President pauses —

Now, what was I saying?

— silence from Klein —

— The President points at the Second CIA Man. —

PRESIDENT

You tell me!

SECOND CIA MAN

I can't say, sir.

PRESIDENT

Tell me!

SECOND CIA MAN

No, sir.

PRESIDENT

Are you disobeying an order?

SECOND CIA MAN

No sir, I'm obeying an order.

PRESIDENT

Whose? Who's giving the orders around here?

ALL CIA MEN

You are, sir.

PRESIDENT

Right! Good! Now we're getting somewhere. . .
And don't call me sir.

ALL CIA MEN

No, sir

PRESIDENT

That's better. Now why did they shoot Chuck?

FIRST CIA MAN

You mean Henry, sir.

PRESIDENT

Listen — I employed him. Don't tell *me* what to
call him.

FIRST CIA MAN

No, sir.

PRESIDENT
— *banging the table slowly* —

No — MR. — PRESIDENT!!!!

FIRST CIA MAN

Yes, Mr. President.

PRESIDENT

Now why did they shoot er — er — er —

FIRST CIA MAN
— *nervously* —

Chuck, sir?

PRESIDENT
– picking his nails –

>I don't like Chuck any more. I'm going to call him
>Arnie — So, why didn't *Arnie* know which country
>he was in?

SECOND CIA MAN

>He'd lost his diary

PRESIDENT

>Did you find it?

The President eyes the group then moves around the desk, knocking over a standard lamp as he does so, and confronts the Men.

FIRST CIA MAN

>Negative, sir.

PRESIDENT

>You found a negative?

FIRST CIA MAN

>No, sir. I was *speaking* in the negative.

PRESIDENT
– to 2nd CIA Man –

>You found it?

FIRST CIA MAN

>He was speaking in the negative too, Mr. President.

PRESIDENT

>You were speaking to me in the negative?

SECOND CIA MAN

>Eh. . . . .?

PRESIDENT

> Now hold it there. There's a photograph of you
> speaking to me, and the negative was in Arnie's
> diary! This is serious.

FIRST CIA MAN

> No it isn't, Mr. President.

PRESIDENT

> Why not?

BLACK CIA MAN

> It doesn't matter sir.

PRESIDENT

> It doesn't matter *Mr. President*

ALL CIA MEN

> It doesn't matter Mr. President.

PRESIDENT

> Then why are you telling me about it? I'm a busy
> man, I am the President of this great country.

ALL CIA MEN

> Yes Sir! Yes Mr. President.

FIRST CIA MAN

> But we weren't telling you about it Mr. President.

PRESIDENT

> You weren't?

ALL CIA MEN

> No, Mr. President.

All the president's men.

PRESIDENT

> Then who was?

FIRST CIA MAN

> Well — *coughs* — it's like this. . .we found this,
> Mr. President.

He carefully opens a folder, holds out to the President a postcard wrapped in a plastic container.

FIRST CIA MAN

> It's very precious, sir.
> It's our only piece of evidence as of this moment
> in time, so far, as of yet. We're having it tested for
> fingerprints later.

The President takes it from him, and roughly tears the plastic container open. He removes the card and examines it closely.

The CIA Men exchange worried looks as the President carelessly drops the plastic wrapper into his coffee.

PRESIDENT
— *reading aloud* —

> "Today Gropinger . . . tomorrow, the world.
> Signed . . . Moriarty."

FIRST CIA MAN

> It has a London, England postmark, sir . . .

The President absentmindedly tears up the note as he thinks.

FIRST CIA MAN

> Sir!

—*he screams* —

PRESIDENT

> What did you call me?

FIRST CIA MAN

> You tore it, Mr. President.

PRESIDENT

> That's better. Now, as I understand the situation, we've got an international crisis situation on our hands here, gentlemen.

The President drops the pieces of the note on the floor and all the CIA Men scrabble for the pieces.

PRESIDENT

> Klein?

FIRST CIA MAN
— looking up from floor —

> Yes, sir.

PRESIDENT

> Get on the first plane to London, France. Keep on top of this situation. I want an every hour on the hour situation report from you.

KLEIN

> Affirmative, Mr. President. Sir.

SCENE 4

INSIDE NEW SCOTLAND YARD. LONDON. TEATIME.

Within the conference room the heads of police for five continents sit around a table. Klein is droning on, each delegate listening through the simultaneous translation earphone system:

> We have to accept a rethink of a whole new methodology to probe out the ongoing re-evaluation of the potential situation, before handling this phase of the operation, at this moment in time to seek out an overly acceptable situation which is not only intrinsically basic as of now, but also operative at this time in a potential let-sleeping-dogs-lie-situation, as of the previously stated, moment in time. Speaking for myself, as of now, this makes the whole goddam shebang acceptable in my book, which refers back to the original hypothesis that . . .

AFRICAN POLICE CHIEF
— listening to jungle drums on his "translation" earphones, gives the Black Power salute and says —

> Right on, Comrade.

KLEIN
— *clearing his throat* —

> As I see it, gentlemen, if we don't make Moriarty
> inoperative, as of now, it's an end-of-civilisation-as-we-
> know-it-situation.

*In the distance Big Ben strikes the quarter hour. The delegates look at their
watches, and when the chime finishes the Englishman speaks:*

> Thank you, Mr. Klein. Does anyone object if I continue in
> English?

— *The Delegates take off their earphones* —

> No? Good. Now, getting down to brass tacks, and to stop
> beating about the bush, with no shilly shallying. . .The
> point is this chap Moriarty has given us five days to give
> him control of the world as we know it. . .and believe me,
> gentlemen, this is no idle threat viz. Gropinger.

*There is a mutter of agreement from all except the Australian who, looking
out of the window, says:*

Now look, wait a moment, who the bleedin' 'ell does this
Moriarty drongo think he is? We gonna take him seriously?

*The Australian is immediately shot dead through the window and falls across
the table destroying the tea service.*

ENGLISHMAN

Ah well. I think that's answered *his* question.

*Everybody except the Englishman hides under the table. The Englishman
immediately presses a button on his table which lowers steel shutters on the
windows and speaks to his secretary:*

Miss Hoskins . . .

MISS HOSKINS

Yes, Charles?

He destroys her with a glance. . .

MISS HOSKINS
— correcting herself —

Sir. . . Sir Charles.

ENGLISHMAN

Inform New Scotland Yard and ring for some more tea.
There's a sniper in Big Ben . . . Uh . . . you can get up now,
gentlemen.

All the delegates get up except for the American, Klein.

KLEIN

What?

ENGLISHMAN

Oh dear . . . er, as of now . . . at this moment in time we are
in a getting-out-from-under-the-table-situation, Mr. Klein.

KLEIN
— getting out from under —

Glad to hear that, Commissioner.

AFRICAN

Dis am not de work of de real late great Professor Moriarty. He been done dead dese damn seventy-five years, bwana.

ENGLISHMAN

You've got a point there, Dr. Schmidt.

— turning to his Secretary —

Ask the computer if Moriarty is still alive Miss Hoskins.

MISS HOSKINS

Yes, sir.

She types out the question on a small computer.

"IS PROFESSOR MORIARTY STILL ALIVE?"

The screen empties and nothing appears.

MISS HOSKINS

It's not working.

ENGLISHMAN

Did you type "please"?

MISS HOSKINS

Sorry.

She types the word: "PLEASE"
The screen fills with one word: "NO"

MISS HOSKINS

It says no!

ENGLISHMAN

Well then, gentlemen, in that case I suggest . . .

The computer chatters noisily. . .

ENGLISHMAN

What's it saying now?

MISS HOSKINS

It says you didn't say "thank you".

ENGLISHMAN

Oh all right, tell it "thank you" and ask it if there really is a
Moriarty.

— She types out the question —

I don't know what we'd do without these marvellous
machines . . . catch somebody I suppose.

The computer retorts:

"IS THERE REALLY A MORIARTY — WHAT?"

ENGLISHMAN
— exasperated —

Good God, who programmed this bloody machine . . .
Barbara Cartland?

On the screen we see . . . "GOOD MANNERS COST NOTHING"

AFRICAN
— joining the group —

We have de way with de computers in my country.

He turns and kicks the machine three times and the screen fills with the
words:

"AAAAAARGH!"

The screen clears and the following appears:

"ALRIGHT! ALRIGHT! YES THERE IS A MORIARTY,
BLIMEY KEEP YOUR HAIR ON!"

KLEIN

Ask it which Moriarty it is.

ENGLISHMAN

— gesturing towards machine —

Miss Hoskins . . .

Miss Hoskins attempts to type but before she can, the frightened machine chatters and produces the answer at high speed:

"HIS ONLY LIVING DESCENDANT (NO OTHER INFORMATION AVAILABLE) SIR!"

AFRICAN
— hitting the computer with a fly-whisk —

Now Mr. Computer, sonny boy sir, you just tell us how we deal with this present day Moriarty rapscallion.

The screen clears and the answer appears:

"SEND FOR PRESENT DAY SHERLOCK HOLMES, C/O Box 221B BAKER STREET."

ENGLISHMAN

I think this is a job for the Chief Commissioner . . .

AFRICAN

Well ah think we have got all de answers we need from dis electric stool pigeon.

He draws his pistol and shoots the computer. . .

The screen fills with the words:

```
"You  d
        i
          r
            t
              y

                r
                  a
                    t
```

SCENE 5

LONDON. BAKER STREET.

A police car, lights flashing and siren sounding, screeches to a halt. The Chief Commissioner jumps out and stops in front of a door which carries the following sign:

A. SHERLOCK HOLMES
PRIVATE INVESTIGATOR
ENQUIRIES WELCOME

Inside Holmes's Waiting Room, his Scottish Housekeeper, Mrs. Hudson, is dusting and spraying the furniture with an aerosol. On seeing the Commissioner, she stops abruptly:

>   Yes, sir?

CHIEF COMMISSIONER

>   I have an appointment with Mr. Holmes. Chief Commissioner Blocker of the Yard.

MRS. HUDSON
– opening the inner office door, polishing it as she does so –

>   Go right in, sir. Mr. Holmes should be back any minute.

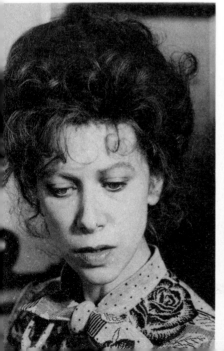

The Chief Commissioner enters and looks around. The Office is shabby and furnished not unlike that of his famous garandfather. It has a few incongruous modern additions. Besides the usual certificates and diplomas, his grandfather's violin hangs on the wall in a glass case. There is also an oil painting of the great Sherlock Holmes. The Chief Commissioner takes all this in, including a tobacco jar with the words Potent Oriental Tobacco written on it in flamboyant lettering. The initials are much larger than the words, so that to the onlooker it reads at first glance P.O.T. The Commissioner sniffs it and reacts violently to the suspicious aroma. Next to it we see a jar labelled Jeffries Old Imperial Nugget Textured Shag. Once again it is the J.O.I.N.T.S. which is most obviously noticeable.

MRS. HUDSON
—noticing his interest, but completely misinterpreting it —

It's redolent with atmosphere, isn't it sir?

CHIEF COMMISSIONER

It certainly is.

He opens another jar — labelled H.A.S.H. (Herbes Au Sherlock Holmes). Meanwhile Mrs. Hudson takes his briefcase and uses her aerosol on it, giving it a brisk polish. In near ecstasy she moans . . .

I love leather. . . Make yourself comfortable, sir. Would you care for some of our "Grand Royal African Special Selection"? It's Mr. Holmes's favourite.

CHIEF COMMISSIONER
— clearing his throat —

Not just now thank you.

Mrs. Hudson gives the briefcase a final rub, puts it down and exits. The Chief Commissioner sits, picks up a copy of the Times and settles back to read. Then, annoyed by a fly, he rolls up the Times and stands, poised to deliver a death blow to the unfortunate insect. Simultaneously, Arthur Sherlock Holmes enters the outer room and catches sight of the Commissioner's shadow through the inner office's frosted glass window. Convinced that an unknown assailant is hiding within, Holmes rushes forth to grapple with the unsuspecting Commissioner. . .

HOLMES

Drop that!

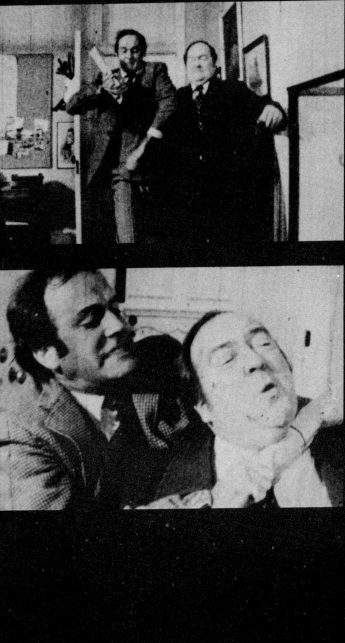

CHIEF COMMISSIONER

Look! Ah! You're hurting my . . .

HOLMES

Drop it or I'll . . .

The newspaper falls to the ground and Holmes expertly kicks it away, before kneeing the Chief Commissioner in the crutch. The Chief Commissioner doubles up and Holmes dashes to the paper, picks it up and turns threateningly towards the Chief Commissioner.

CHIEF COMMISSIONER
— in despair —

Holmes look, no!

Holmes hits him twice across the head with the paper and then puts the Chief Commissioner in an arm lock, gripping him from behind and holding the rolled Times across the Chief Commissioner's throat as though it were a knife.

HOLMES

Don't move, my friend. I warn you, I shan't hesistate to use this.

Behind them the door opens and Mrs. Hudson enters. . .

MRS HUDSON

Oh Mr. Holmes, I forgot to say you have a visitor. It's . . .

HOLMES
—interrupting her and still holding the Chief Commissioner fast, he screams out:

Well tell him to wait. Can't you see I'm working on a case.

MRS. HUDSON
— staring in total disbelief:

That's your visitor, you great clown.

Then, hitting Holmes hard across the head with her hand, she continues:

Pull yourself together, it's the Chief Commissioner for Scotland Yard, you ninny.

Holmes, thrown off balance by his housekeeper's blow, falls to the floor, shaking the stars from before his eyes in a desperate attempt to regain some decorum. . .

HOLMES

Thank *you. Thank* you, Mrs. Hudson, that'll be all.

— and, turning to the dishevelled Police Commissioner —

My dear sir. . .

MRS. HUDSON

— poking her head around the door to make a final assault on Holmes's ego —

And get up! I only pressed those trousers yesterday.

HOLMES

— hissing through his teeth —

That'll be ALL. Thank you.

Holmes scrambles to his feet and turns once again to the Commissioner, all cordiality:

Commissioner, pray forgive my rather unorthodox
greeting. I fear I. . .took you for an intruder. Are you
recovered?

CHIEF COMMISSIONER

A little shaken, Holmes, but none the worse, thank you. . .

— and then, fast as lightning, he knees Holmes in the crutch, to cackle —

Got you, you stupid bastard!

Holmes, in agony and once more on the floor, raises two crossed fingers and acquiesces to the philosophy of an eye-for-an-eye:

HOLMES

Fair do's, Commissioner. Pax and pray be seated

The Chief Commissioner sits.

Would you forgive me for one moment if I moaned?

CHIEF COMMISSIONER

Of course.

HOLMES
— moans . . . —

Now, perhaps

— he starts crawling towards a suitable chair —

you would be so kind as to tell me to what good fortune
I owe the pleasure of this visit?

The door is opened by Mrs. Hudson.

MRS. HUDSON

You moaned, sir?

HOLMES

It's nothing thank you, Mrs. Hudson.

MRS. HUDSON
— making reference to a family weakness for anaesthetic narcotics —

You wouldn't care for some of your special sniffing salts.

HOLMES

That'll be all, thank you, Mrs. Hudson.
Now, Commissioner, I assume you are here as the emissary
of a personage so eminent that his identity must remain
a secret, even to me?

CHIEF COMMISSIONER
— nodding —

The Prime Minister himself.

HOLMES

And on a matter of gravest national importance, which
has baffled the finest minds in five continents and a failure
to find a rapid solution to an impending crisis which would

plunge this country into the most desperately perilous situation.

CHIEF COMMISSIONER

Exactly.

HOLMES

Sounds pretty straightforward. Would you care for some tea?

CHIEF COMMISSIONER

Oh, thank you.

HOLMES
— still in pain, Holmes makes to crawl towards the door, then —

You wouldn't prefer something a little more illegal?

CHIEF COMMISSIONER

Not while I'm on duty, Mr. Holmes, no. . . it may intrigue you to know, sir, that this business concerns a descendant of your grandfather's most notorious enemy.

Holmes has reached the door and turns dramatically.

HOLMES

Moriarty!

At this moment, the door flies open, catches Holmes a ghastly blow across the head, and knocks him to the floor once more. Watson enters jovially and unperceptively.

WATSON

Holmes! Holmes! Cooee, I'm home. . .

— then, seeing the Chief Commissioner —

Oh, good afternoon.

— and as his eyes alight upon the supine figure of his master —

Good Lord! Are you looking for something, Holmes?

HOLMES
— an acid reply —

No I am *not* looking for something, Watson.

WATSON

Good Lord! Good Lord!!! You're bleeding. Are you all
right?

HOLMES
– taking Watson by the arm –

Just a gash, Watson. Just a *gaping* wound.

WATSON

Good Lord.

HOLMES

Commissioner, may I introduce my trusted friend and colleague, Dr. Watson, grandson of the celebrated. . .

CHIEF COMMISSIONER

How do you do, Dr. Watson.

WATSON

How do you do, Commissionaire. And which cinema do you work at?

CHIEF COMMISSIONER

What?

WATSON
– his attention taken by the blood flowing down from Holmes's temple –

Did you cut yourself shaving, Holmes? You should put some Sellotape on that. *I am* a doctor you know.

Holmes takes Watson by the arm and leads him to a chair. He begins to explain:

HOLMES

The Commissioner of *police* is about to outline a case for us, Watson.

WATSON

Good Lord!

HOLMES

It concerns none other than the infamous Professor
Moriarty.

WATSON

Moriarty!

Watson leaps up holding his walking stick threateningly, alert for danger.

HOLMES

Watson . . .

CHIEF COMMISSIONER

Let me explain, Dr. . .

WATSON

That devil!!

HOLMES

Watson . . .

WATSON

Good Lord. Thank God!! We soon sorted that one out,
Holmes, eh?

HOLMES
– to the Chief Commissioner –

You may speak freely in front of Dr. Watson,
Commissioner. He is my most trusted friend and associate.
Besides that, he understands very little.

WATSON
– with great feeling –

Thank you, Holmes.

                                        HOLMES

                                        He is.

WATSON

I thought he was dead, Holmes.

HOLMES
— to the Commissioner —

You see.

CHIEF COMMISSIONER

Yes — You have no doubt read, Mr. Holm. . .

WATSON

Good Lord!

CHIEF COMMISSIONER

. . . read in the newspapers recently . . .

WATSON

Great Scott.

He now looks at Holmes who waves him quiet with a calming gesture. Holmes looks back to the Chief Commissioner.

CHIEF COMMISSIONER

. . . of various mysterious incidents.

HOLMES
— enumerating them on his fingers —

The unexpected but accurate bisecting of the Belgian Foreign Minister, the Royal College of Neddlework Massacre, the strange affair of the seven boiled Bishops and the man-eating poodles of Lambeth Palace enigma.

CHIEF COMMISSIONER

No.

WATSON

Good Lord.

HOLMES

Just as I thought.

CHIEF COMMISSIONER

I am referring to the mysterious shooting of Dr. Gropinger. Holmes, we believe this to be the work of one man.

WATSON

Good Lord.

HOLMES

Shut up!

WATSON

Yes, Holmes.

CHIEF COMMISSIONER
— producing from an envelope the now stuck-together postcard —

This is all we have to go on. A note found in Dr. Gropinger's plane.

HOLMES
— his eyes flashing across the writing —

Moriarty!

WATSON
— leaping to his feet again, stick raised —

Where?!

HOLMES
— showing him the note in his hand, wearily —

Here!

Watson brings his stick down, smashing the note from Holmes's hand.

WATSON

The swine.

HOLMES

So Moriarty has given Civilisation as we know it, five days to live?

'So Moriarty has given civilisation as we know it, five days to live?'

WATSON

Good Lord! How on earth do you know that, Holmes?

HOLMES

It says so here.

WATSON

Amazing. You never cease to astound me, Holmes . . .

CHIEF COMMISSIONER

Our computer tells us this Moriarty is the only living descendant of the professor.

The Chief Commissioner now rises.

We have a conference at the Yard within the hour. Will you be there?

HOLMES

I shall. With Dr. Watson of course.

CHIEF COMMISSIONER

Oh.

Holmes takes the Chief Commissioner's arm confidentially as they walk to the door. And Watson, aware that something private is being said, hovers in the hope he may pick up something.

HOLMES

He's not a brainbox, but he's loyal, trustworthy and brave as a lion. Also . . . he's partly bionic.

CHIEF COMMISSIONER
— amazed —

Bionic?!

HOLMES

Just his nose and his legs. But if there's any tracking to be done, he's our man.

Watson simpers, taps his nose knowingly, and shakes a leg.

CHIEF COMMISSIONER

I see. Good day, Holmes.

HOLMES

Good day, Commissioner.

The Chief Commissioner departs.

Right, Watson, the chase is on and the game's afoot.

At this moment the Commissioner stumbles back through the door making a
strange, choking noise. Watson is first to make a move, striding confidently
forward with his diagnosis . . .

WATSON
He's choking, Holmes. I've seen this before in the Middle
East.

— he begins to bang the Commissioner on the back —

Come on, cough it up and you'll feel better.

— he gives the Commissioner a hearty thump, and replies to the poor man's
screams with —

It's all right, I am a doctor you know.

The Chief Commissioner groans and slumps forward on his knees, before
collapsing altogether to present to the gaping duo a long knife protruding from
his back . . .

HOLMES

Watson! Look!!

WATSON

Good Lord!

HOLMES

He's been stabbed, Watson.

WATSON

Good Lord!! How do you know that, Holmes?

HOLMES

. . . Well, he's got a knife sticking in his back hasn't he?

WATSON

Amazing. Your powers of deduction never cease to ast . . .

HOLMES
— examining the Chief Commissioner —

It hasn't penetrated far though. He'll live all right.

WATSON

Thank God!

HOLMES

The assailant must have . . . wait here, Watson!!

With one bound Holmes is in the corridor and Watson is left with the body. As he kneels, Mrs. Hudson comes in with the tea.

MRS. HUDSON

Your tea, Dr. Watson.

WATSON

Oh.

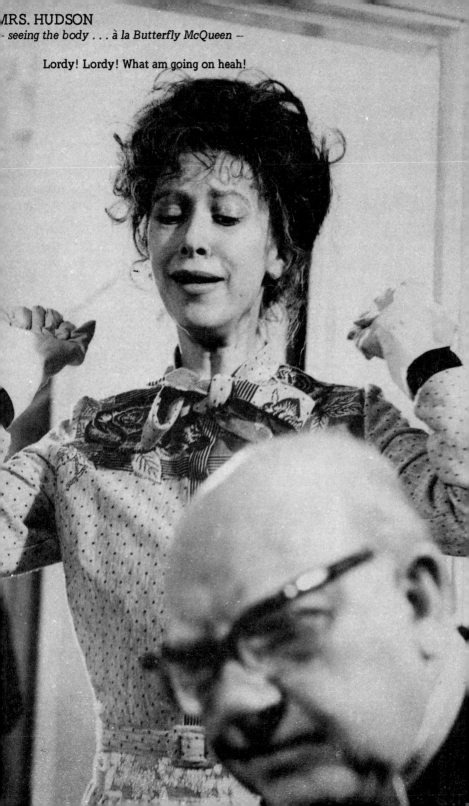

MRS. HUDSON
- *seeing the body . . . à la Butterfly McQueen* —

Lordy! Lordy! What am going on heah!

WATSON

Cut the coon talk, Mrs. Hudson, we've got a stabbing on our hands.

MRS. HUDSON

Good Lord!

WATSON

That's just what I said, Mrs. Hudson. My very words.

— he puts his hand on the knife —

MRS. HUDSON

Is he . . . dead?

WATSON

No. I'll just . . .

— he pulls the knife out —

MRS. HUDSON

. . . But! . . .

WATSON

There!

— shows Mrs. Hudson the extracted knife —

MRS. HUDSON

But that'll kill him.

WATSON

What?

MRS. HUDSON

If you pull the knife out you allow the haemorrhaging to start. Tch tch tch tch.

— she leave the room shaking her head —

WATSON
— staring after her for a moment —

. . . Good Lord. She's right!

Incredibly, Watson starts putting the knife back into the wound. It doesn't re-insert at all easily and the Chief Commissioner does a lot of moaning.

Sorry, old man, but it's for your own good. Don't worry . . . I am a doctor.

He gives the knife a final thump and the Chief Commissioner clearly dies. Watson listens to heart.

Hallo? Hallo?

Watson now looks up and sees Holmes standing by the door looking down at him. Watson leaps to his feet.

Oh hallo, Holmes! He's taken a turn for the worse I'm afraid. He's terribly ill. In fact, Holmes, he's so desperatley ill, he's dead.

HOLMES

The knife was removed and then re-inserted in an attempt to stop the haemorrhaging caused by its removal. The second insertion was the cause of death.

WATSON

Good Lord. How do you know that, Holmes?

HOLMES

I was watching you, I couldn't believe my eyes.

— Then, incredulously shaking his head at Watson —

I leave you alone with the top policeman in Great Britain for thirty seconds and you kill him.

WATSON

I'm very sorry, Holmes.

HOLMES

Sorry isn't good enough.

— he walks to a desk —

WATSON

Oh *no*, Holmes!

HOLMES

If this isn't worth six of the best. . . .

Holmes has taken the cane out of a drawer and turns to Watson.

WATSON

Oh well. . .beat me on my legs Holmes, please.

HOLMES

No, I'm going to beat you on a *non*-bionic part of your body.

WATSON

No you're not.

— he starts to take evasive action —

HOLMES

Yes I am.

— he pursues relentlessly —

WATSON

No you're not.

HOLMES

Yes I am.

WATSON

No you're not.

HOLMES

Yes I am. Yes I am. Yes I am.

Suddenly, Watson, putting in motion his bionic powers, runs like greased lightning out of the room, down the stairs and into the street. Holmes can only shout after him:

I'll get you struck off even more than you are already!

Disturbed by the commotion, Mrs Hudson appears through the kitchen door, calmly drying a violin with a tea towel. Holmes, with more urgent matters at hand than chasing the bionic phenomenon down Baker Street, invokes his housekeeper's assistance:

Ah, there you are — I'd better get the Commissioner down to Forensics. Give me a hand, will you?

Mrs. Hudson, realising the importance of the situation, hurls the instrument into the sink and makes herself ready.

SCENE 6

DOWNSTAIRS IN A LONDON BUS.

To all intents and purposes it is a normal bus with its normal quota of passengers — all being either Arab, West Indian, Pakistani, or Chinese. All, that is, except for Holmes and Watson who are seated beside the door with the parcelled corpse of the Chief Commissioner between them. Holmes sucks his pipe, a blissful expression across his face, while Watson tries desperately to look casually unconcerned. The Conductor, a West Indian, arrives:

Fares please.

WATSON

Two to New Scotland Yard, please.

CONDUCTOR

What you mean "two". What about him?

— nodding at the parcel —

WATSON

Who?

CONDUCTOR

Him!

— pointing to the Commissioner —

WATSON

Oh. The parcel.

CONDUCTOR

No the passenger in the brown paper suit.

WATSON

No, no, it's a parcel, believe me.

CONDUCTOR
— prodding the parcel as he speaks —

"Oh dear. It's brown
paper wrapped around
something."

Hey, come on out and pay your fare like a man, man.

WATSON

No look! Er . . . it may look like a man but in actual fact
it . . . isn't.

CONDUCTOR

Then what it is?

Watson nudges Holmes, desperate for help.

*Watson gives up his attempt to rouse Holmes, who is quite literally, thanks
to the contents of his pipe, in another world.*

WATSON

Oh dear.
It's brown paper wrapped round something.

CONDUCTOR

What?

WATSON

A sort of er . . . model of the Chief Commissioner of
Scotland Yard. It doesn't work any more and so I'm taking
it back. Sort of . . .

CONDUCTOR

Oh ho ho. Pull the other one, it got the bell ringers all over
it.

— he puts hand on the parcel —

WATSON
— trying desperately to stop him —

No really . . .

CONDUCTOR

I'm goin' to inspect this model of yours.

WATSON
— *in near panic* —

No please, Holmes!

Watson looks again to Holmes, who is still looking serene, puffing his pipe.

WATSON

Oh Dear! Please look! er . . .

Watson freezes as the conductor tears some paper round the top of the parcel revealing a grotesque bloodstained dead head. The Conductor peers at it amazed.

WATSON

Oh all right. *Three* to Scotland Yard.

CONDUCTOR

Wait a moment. He am dead!!

WATSON

It doesn't matter. I'll pay for him.

CONDUCTOR

He am *dead!*

WATSON
— *convinced that now they are in it right up to their necks* —

Oh dear . . .

CONDUCTOR

So he goes *under the stairs* because he am a parcel.

WATSON

What?

CONDUCTOR

So . . . that's two to Scotland Yard.

— *he starts moving the parcel towards the compartment under the stairs* —

WATSON
— *intervening* —

Here, show a little respect for the parcel.

CONDUCTOR

Now listen to me, honky, I's de boss on dis bus I can do
anything I like ting-ting, I can throw you off, I can
put all of you under the stairs, I can kill you all with my
bare hands . . . or if you play your cards right, I can marry
the pair of you.

WATSON

Holmes . . .

The Conductor now turns his attention to the smoking Holmes.

CONDUCTOR

Hey you! No smoking on the lower deck.

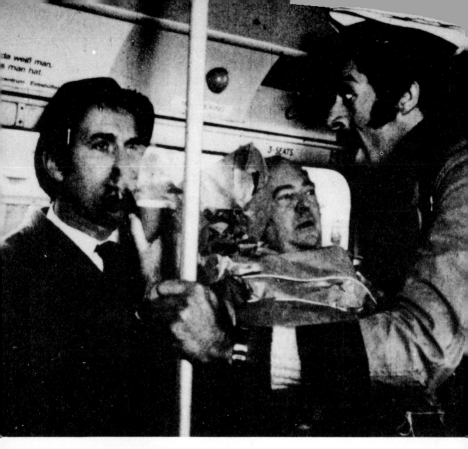

— *pointing at parcel* —

     He goes under the stairs and
— *pointing to Holmes* —

     you go upstairs.

HOLMES

     It's all right, Conductor, it's not tobacco.

CONDUCTOR
— *reacts . . . then, eyes glinting in anticipation* —

     Oh ho. You got the certain susbstances eh? In that case,
     you should be up front with *him*.

The Conductor's pointing finger leads the sleuth's eyes towards the Driver's compartment. Had they ever wondered at the tedium of driving a London bus day in day out, such concern is allayed forthwith at the sight of the glazed-eyed driver puffing blissfully at his "naughty" cigarette.

SCENE 7

NEW SCOTLAND YARD. A SMALL RECEPTION ROOM.

Behind the reception desk a policeman watches Holmes and Watson carry the parcelled Commissioner up to him:

> Yes?

HOLMES
— eagerly passing the buck, and making for the nearest door —

> You just deal with this, Watson. Er, I'll go ahead and tell them we're here.

WATSON

> Er . . . um . . . er

DESK SGT.
— glaring at the unlikely duo —

> Yes ? ? ?

WATSON

> Would you tell the Commissioner's secretary that he's back from lunch, and now he wants to go down to Forensics.

DESK SGT.

> Why would he want to go down there?

WATSON

> I think he fancies having a bit of a post mortem.

Watson scampers after Holmes, leaving the P.C. staring after him.

DESK SGT.

> It takes all sorts of people!

— then, staring closely at the parcel, he sees the Commissioner's face —

> Hallo!

— standing erect and saluting —

> Excuse me, sir. I've got bad news. I'm very much afraid
> you're dead . . . however I would like to take this opportu-
> nity to tell you how much we've all enjoyed working under
> you all these years. I'm sure your secretary if she was here
> would join me in wishing you all you would wish
> yourself up there in the great police state in the sky. . .
> furthermore . . .

SCENE 8

SCOTLAND YARD. CONFERENCE ROOM.

*We see the representatives (of America, Asia, Africa, and Europe) sitting
around the conference table. There is a tea lady pouring tea from her trolley.
The Englishman addresses them:*

> Gentlemen, Mr. Holmes and Dr. Watson will be with us in a
> moment. The purpose of this meeting is to agree upon a
> plan, a plan which will enable us to move against Moriarty.
> Remember, gentlemen, this fiend will stop at nothing.

A "Mmmmm" of apprehension and agreement spreads around the room.

ENGLISHMAN

> Your suggestions, gentlemen.

AFRICAN

> Ah suggest we do nothing.

ENGLISHMAN

> Nothing?

AFRICAN

> Nothing.

KLEIN

> Nothing? ? !

AFRICAN

Exactly. We all know that this madman, this international bedbug, will stop at nothing. So if we do nothing, perhaps he will stop at it.

CHINESE

Clever. Very Clever!

KLEIN

Now wait a moment. At this moment of time, as of now. . . you mean he won't stop at anything so if we do anything, it's not going to stop him?

AFRICAN

On de button.

AUSTRALIAN

Hey, that's good. You cunning old abbo, you.

—The African punches him —

ENGLISHMAN

Gentlemen. . .er. . .

KLEIN

It's an old trick, Superintendent, but it might just work!

ENGLISHMAN

Yes, I think you're taking me too literally.

CHINESE

Please. Expose flaw in argument. He will stop at nothing so . . .

ENGLISHMAN

Wait a moment . . . he will stop at *nothing*, so if we do *something* . . . no . . . that *can't* be right.

KLEIN

If we do something, he won't stop . . . so we must do
absolutely nothing.

CHINESE

Wait. How will he *know* we are doing nothing?

AUSTRALIAN

We'll announce it. At a big press conference.

ENGLISHMAN

But . . . he'll never *believe* us!

KLEIN

On the other hand if we announce we're doing something,
he may suspect we're lying . . . and *stop!*

AFRICAN

Sounds pretty good to me!

The Intercom on the table blurts out:

Mr. Holmes and Dr. Watson, sir.

ENGLISHMAN

Show them in please.

Holmes and Watson are shown in and introduced:

ENGLISHMAN

Mr. Holmes, may I introduce Julius Klein from the FBI

Klein and Holmes slap their hands together in a cool hippy-style greeting.

ENGLISHMAN

Foo Tong of Peking

In faultless Chinese, Holmes conducts a traditional greeting and turns to meet Superintendent McClennan from Australia who, as is explained to him, has just arrived to replace his unfortunate colleague shot the day before. As McClennan makes to slap Holmes's back in traditional Aussie-style greeting, a shot rings out and the Superintendent falls dead . . .

WATSON

charges towards the open window, leans out and shouts:

Good Lord! Look!

At which point the Englishman presses a button to close the steel window shutters and shouts:

Quick. Down!

Unable to extricate himself in time, Watson's neck is pinned to the window-ledge. Unaware of the soft gurgling emanating from the fearless Doctor, the Englishman surveys the scene.

Everyone all right?

CHINESE

Apart from . . .

— he indicates the Australian who is lying dead —

ENGLISHMAN

Oh dear. Could one of you possibley tell them? They were furious about the first one.

Klein points at the absurd sight of Watson's flaying legs.

He's trapped!

The Englishman makes straight for the button to release the steel shutters, and as he does so Watson pops out just in time to miss another of the sniper's bullets which plummets instead into the unfortunate Chinaman.
Once again the Englishman presses the button to close the shutters, this time on the Doctor's fingers. Watson howls, but all attention is focused on the Chinaman who staggers around the table choking. Each of the delegates takes an arm, a shoulder, and other parts of his anatomy that present themselves. He makes a couple of quick, convulsive steps and collapses dramatically on the table, pressing the shutter button as he does so. Once more the shutters go up, releasing Watson's fingers, and the inevitable shot finds its mark on the African . . .

KLEIN

Shut the shutters!!

He hurls himself at the table and presses the button. The shutters start to descend; bullets perforate the tea urn and the tea lady. She dies with a scream.

KLEIN

Superintendent, for God's sake *do* something about that sniper.

ENGLISHMAN
– who is calmly filling his cup from the perforated urn –

Are you panicking, Klein?

KLEIN

Panicking!? He's been out there for SIX HOURS.

ENGLISHMAN
– adding sugar and milk –

Rome wasn't built in a day, Klein.

KLEIN

Are you going to do something or . . .

ENGLISHMAN

Oh very well, I'll remind them. But we're busy today.

— he picks up the Intercom —

KLEIN

Busy?

ENGLISHMAN

The Queen's got one of her lunches on.

KLEIN

I have never seen such incredible incompetence, such mind-boggling inefficiency, such typically British . . .

ENGLISHMAN

Now you listen to me!

He leans forward determinedly, unwittingly putting his hand on the vital button.

KLEIN

No you listen to me !!! Typically British . . .

Suddenly he looks towards the window and registers fear . . .

Oh . . . No!

The inevitable shot finds its mark and Klein expires.

ENGLISHMAN

That'll learn him. Crikey.

— he looks around —

He's going through us like a dose of salts isn't he?

HOLMES

Yes. Well I suggest we agree a plan while there are still some
of us left.

WATSON

Good idea, Holmes!

HOLMES

How about a convention . . . to which we invite the
world's most distinguished detectives . . . it would be a
dreadful temptation to try to kill them all off at one fell
swoop.

WATSON

Steady on, Holmes. You wouldn't actually try to do that
would you?

HOLMES

No *I* wouldn't Watson, no. But Moriarty would.

WATSON

Good Lord! He would too, the devil!

HOLMES

And when he shows his hand . . .

— snaps fingers —

SCENE 9

INSIDE THE WHITE HOUSE.

*The new President, looking just like the last one except for his glasses and his
hair which is blond, is removing his predecessor's portrait from the wall
and replacing it with his own. He is helped in his task by two CIA Men, one
black and one white, to whom he now turns:*

> There, gentlemen. Everything's going to be *different* from
> now on.

*Having so said, he turns round knocking over a Golden Eagle (symbol of the
Republic).*

WHITE CIA MAN
— who rushes to pick it up —

> Allow me, sir . . .

PRESIDENT

> Allow me . . . what?

WHITE CIA MAN

> Allow me to pick up the eagle, sir.

PRESIDENT
— loudly —

> Allow me to pick up the eagle . . .

— he bangs the desk knocking over a tray of glasses —

> . . . Mr. President!

*The Black CIA Man who has started to pick up the tray and the glasses, is also
set upon:*

PRESIDENT

> And what are *you* doing?

BLACK CIA MAN

> Picking up the glasses, sir.

PRESIDENT

— *exasperated* —

> Picking up the glasses . . . *Mr. President!*

BLACK CIA MAN

> Sorry, sir.

PRESIDENT

> Can't you get it into your heads that there's a new administration in this country?

BOTH CIA MEN

> Yes, Mr. President, sir.

WHITE CIA MAN

> But . . .

PRESIDENT

> But what?

WHITE CIA MAN

> The former President also always required us to address him as Mr. President, sir.

PRESIDENT

— *banging the table* —

> Mr. President, Mr. President.

WHITE CIA MAN

> What?

PRESIDENT

> I said, Mr. President, Mr. President.

WHITE CIA MAN

> Yes . . . Mr. President, Mr. President.

PRESIDENT

What did you say?

WHITE CIA MAN

I said Mr. President, Mr. President . . . Mr. President.

PRESIDENT

What are you saying Mr. President Mr. President
Mr. President for?

WHITE CIA MAN

I'm not quite sure . . . Mr. President Mr. President.

PRESIDENT

Why are you calling me Mr. President Mr. President now?

WHITE CIA MAN

I don't know, sir.

PRESIDENT

Thank God we got that sorted out. Now what do we have
to discuss this morning?

BLACK CIA MAN

The end-of-Civilization-as-we-know-it situation, sir.

The President eyes him.

Uh . . . Mr. President . . .

PRESIDENT

What end-of-Civilization-as-we-know-it situation?

BLACK CIA MAN

The end-of-Civilization-as-we-know-it situation.

PRESIDENT

> Well you'll have to fill me in on that . . . I've been fighting
> an erection.

WHITE CIA MAN

> There's a man called Moriarty threatening to end Civiliza-
> tion as we know it.

PRESIDENT

> What?

BLACK CIA MAN

> And we've only two days left, sir.

PRESIDENT

> And we've only two days left . . .

*— he jumps up and down rhythmically as he stresses the all-important
words —*

> *Mr. President!*

BOTH CIA MEN

— looking at each other —

> Yes . . . we've only two days left . . .

— they jump up and down likewise —

> *Mr. President!*

PRESIDENT

> What are you guys doing?

BOTH CIA MEN

> We thought you wanted us to jump, sir.

PRESIDENT

> If I want you to jump I'll say jump.

He turns his attention to a dossier on his desk.

Now what's the situation on this situation?

WHITE CIA MAN

There's been an international Police conference in London, England to discuss options . . . Mr. President.

PRESIDENT

And what happened?

BLACK CIA MAN

We lost six men.

PRESIDENT

Six? Six men eh . . . well that's acceptable. Go on . . .

WHITE CIA MAN

There's to be another conference, sir . . .

The President reacts.

ALL (PRESIDENT INCLUDED)

There's to be another conference . . .

— jumping in unison —

Mr. President!

PRESIDENT

Did I say jump?

BOTH CIA MEN

No, sir.

They realise their mistake too late.

PRESIDENT
— shouting —

No ...

He jumps in the air. The CIA Men do likewise.

ALL (PRESIDENT INCLUDED)

Mr. President!!

PRESIDENT

Good. Now what sort of another conference?

WHITE CIA MAN

A conference of all the greatest detectives in the world ...
Mr. President.

PRESIDENT

Hasn't that been done before?

BLACK CIA MAN

Not as well as we're going to do it, sir.

SCENE 10

A HOTEL FOYER. THE LAST DAY BEFORE THE END OF CIVILISATION AS WE KNOW IT.

Hercule Poirot's head appears over the Reception Desk to say:

> Excusez-moi mais je m'appelle Poirot. Est-ce-qu'il y a personne qui parle Francais?

The receptionist stares blankly in reply, and Poirot persists:

Qui parle Francais ici?

Met with the same blank expression, Poirot shouts:

Qui parle Francais?

The smiling face of Mrs Hudson appears as from nowhere, and from her lips there comes a sensual

Je!

SCENE 11

THE HOTEL TEA ROOM.

In the company of a few scattered guests and a sombre string trio, Dr. Watson sits and waits. Shortly, Mrs. Hudson appears with a tray of tea:

> Your tea, Dr. Watson. I prepared it myself. I've put some-
> thing in it for the *inner* man.

WATSON

> Thank you, Mrs. Hudson.

He milks and sugars his tea. She sits beside him at his table.

MRS. HUDSON

> Mr. Hercule Parrot has just arrived. I've made him
> comfortable.

WATSON

> Good show.

— he takes a sip of the tea —

> Good Lord . . . rather good.

— he takes another sip —

> Whatever did you slip in here?

MRS. HUDSON

> Drambuie. . .washing soda. . .and a snifter of TCP. It's an
> old Highland sheep dip recipe.

WATSON

> Really!

— he searches for his notebook —

> I must make a note of that. . .Tell my doctor in the
> morning.

"It's a disguise, Watson"

"Would it be Prince Philip, sir?"

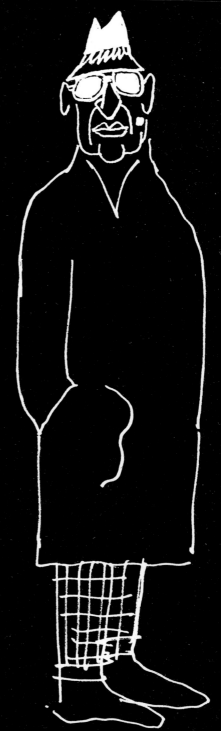

MRS. HUDSON

Here they come now.

WATSON
— surprised, looks around —

Already? . . . Oh . . .

At the tea room door Holmes, disguised as Kojak, has appeared. He is some way away and looks around casually. Spotting him, Watson shouts:

Holmes! Over here, Holmes! Cooee! Holmes? Here we are Holmes. . .can you hear me?

HOLMES
— outraged that Watson could be such a fool as to blow the gaff —

Coming, Watson. . .coming.

He has to walk across the tea room to Watson and Mrs. Hudson. As he does so he turns up the collar of his ill-fitting Kojak raincoat in a futile attempt to remain inconspicuous.

Pound to a penny Moriarty has this place under surveillance.

WATSON

Good Lord! Of course . . . I see, yes . . . but why are you dressed like that, Holmes?

HOLMES

It's a disguise, Watson.

WATSON

Good Lord.

— peering at his colleague —

So it is. It's jolly good, isn't it, Mrs. Hudson?

MRS. HUDSON

I'm not sure . . . Who is it supposed to be, sir?

HOLMES

It's . . .

WATSON
— *interrupting like a schoolboy playing a party game* —

No, don't tell us. Let's *guess*.

MRS. HUDSON

Would it be Prince Philip, sir?

HOLMES

At least you got the nationality right, Mrs. Hudson.

WATSON

. . . is it a man, Holmes?

HOLMES

Of course it's a man, Watson.

WATSON

I know Holmes . . . it's you!

HOLMES

No it is not me. It's Kojak!

WATSON
— *he looks around* —

Where?

Holmes grabs him and points to himself.

HOLMES

Here!

In the manner of Kojak he pinches Watson's cheek and shows him a lollipop.

Who loves ya baby? Eh Watson? Eh? Kojak!

MRS. HUDSON

Oh *Kojak!* The camera people . . . I didn't know they were Greeks . . .

HOLMES

No, Mrs. Hudson. Kojak! The detective on television.

MRS. HUDSON

Oh . . .
Well. . .I hope you didn't pay a lot of money for it, sir. . .It's not terribly convincing.

HOLMES

It was the only one they had . . .

MRS. HUDSON

Well I'd take it back if I were you, sir. It's a disgrace . . .

HOLMES

Yes thank you, Mrs. Hudson . . . That'll be all . . .

MRS. HUDSON

They ought to be ashamed . . . charging people good money for trash like that . . .

HOLMES

Thank you, Mrs. Hudson. That will be all!

MRS. HUDSON

Wicked. . .

HOLMES

Quiet! Mrs. Hudson. . .

MRS. HUDSON

Oh you puir wee soul . . . you've been duped. . .tut tut . . .
just like taking sweeties from a child, so it is. . .

HOLMES

Thank you. . . .would you let me know when the guests
have arrived, Mrs. Hudson? Come along, Watson. . . There's
not a moment to lose. . .

*He begins to remove his disguise as he strides purposefully on, followed by
Watson and watched by the still tut-tutting Mrs. Hudson. As Watson passes
the hotel 'phone booth, be catches a glimpse of Superman changing for
ACTION.*

SCENE 12

THE HOTEL CAR PARK.

*A large beaten up car approaches the hotel forecourt and breaks down as it
comes to its destination, smoke belching from beneath the bonnet. Lieuten-
ant Columbo alights, dressed as usual in a beaten up old raincoat. The Hotel
Commissionaire eyes him suspiciously. Looking curiously at him and scrat-
ching his head, Columbo passes the Commissionaire a grimy card. . .*

Er. . .Have it fixed and get my wife to pick it up, will ya?

Without a second glance at the heap of metal in the forecourt, Columbo enters the hotel, smoking his small cigar.

SCENE 13

THE STAIRS OF THE HOTEL.

WATSON

    Good idea, Holmes. . .Brilliant!!

HOLMES

    What?!

WATSON

    Your idea about going upstairs. . . Brilliant!

HOLMES

Must you always get so ecstatic about everything I do?

WATSON

By jove that's a good question. That's a hard one. What's the answer, Holmes?

SCENE 14

The hotel forecourt with its Commissionaire are busy today. . .Another car, this one with number plate JB 007, pulls in. Contrary to expectations, however, the man in the car is "M", the beautiful girl "companion", Miss Moneypacket. . .

Keep ticking over Miss Moneypacket, this'll only take a moment.

MISS MONEYPACKET
— kissing him lovingly —

Stay cool, "M" baby.

A swift double-take and "M" extricates himself from her embrace, straightens his tie, and walks stiff-legged past the Commissionaire into the hotel.

SCENE 15

THE TOP OF THE STAIRS OF THE HOTEL.

HOLMES

It's only 4.53. Quick, Watson! Get a crossword! There are
several moments to lose.

WATSON

Do you really think Moriarty will come, Holmes?

HOLMES

Of course. Do you think he could resist a challenge like this,
Watson?

WATSON

What's he going to look like?

HOLMES

We don't know, Watson. We just don't know. He could
come as any one of them.

McGARRIT

Hello Dano, just arrived safely in Limeyland — over. . .

SCENE 16

THE HOTEL LOBBY.

Steve McGarrit is looking around the Foyer. He speaks into his walkie talkie.

McGARRIT

McGarrit here, patch me through to FIVE-O.

We hear atmospheric noises coming from the walkie talkie as he waits.

DISTORT VOICE
— from walkie talkie —

Five-O here, Steve.

Watson appears behind him and hits him on the head with a blackjack. He falls senseless to the ground and Watson picks up the walkie talkie. . .

WATSON

. . . and out!

He drags McGarrit off into the death room.

SCENE 17

HOTEL — THE UPSTAIRS ROOM.

HOLMES

He's a master of disguise, Watson.

WATSON

I bet he is too. The devil!

HOLMES

There's just one way to recognise him Watson — he has an unmistakable high-pitched laugh — I heard it once in the Odeon at Kabul.

WATSON

Good Lord. . . but how are you going to get him to laugh Holmes?

HOLMES

I have an emergency joke Watson, prepared for me by the Special Branch. It's what they call a SOLID GOLD WHOOFER! — now, give me a clue!

WATSON

I don't know any solid gold whoofers, Holmes.

HOLMES
— *wearily* —

No, Watson — from the crossword.

WATSON

Oh sorry, Holmes. . .er. . .one across: "Simple source of citrus fruit. . ." One, five and four.

HOLMES

. . .Elementary, my dear Watson.

WATSON

What?

HOLMES

A lemon tree, my dear Watson.

WATSON

That's clever, Holmes.

SCENE 18

THE HOTEL LOBBY ONCE MORE.

Watson with Sam Spade (or is it Phillip Marlowe?) in white 40s raincoat, and Fedora.

SPADE
— *pointing at a guest list* —

I'm down there, sweetheart — that's me.

WATSON

Ah yes . . . Mr. *Spode.*

SPADE

Let's call a Spade a Spade, shall we?

WATSON

Sorry.

— opening the door of the death room and allowing Spade in —

Okay blue eyes, this is the end of the line for you.

SPADE
— incredulous —

That's terrible. That's the worst impersonation of me I have ever . . .

Watson shoots him between the eyes.

SPADE

Nice shooting, Watson baby . . . you lousy mimic you.

SCENE 19

HOTEL — THE UPSTAIRS ROOM.

WATSON

Two down. "Conservative pays ex-wife maintenance." Seven and four.

HOLMES

Elementary, my dear Watson.

WATSON

What?

HOLMES

. . . Alimony Tory, my dear Watson.

WATSON

By jove that's good.

SCENE 20

THE HOTEL LOBBY *YET AGAIN.*

*Watson with Poirot. With the inevitability of a lemming to the precipice, he
leads Poirot through the death room door.*

> This way, Mr. Parrot

Drawing his sabre, Watson follows him in. . .

> Who's a pretty boy then?

Without one ruffled feather, Watson disposes neatly of his prey.

SCENE 21

HOTEL – THE UPSTAIRS ROOM.

WATSON

> Three down. "Southern California style." One, two and eight.

HOLMES

> . . .A la Monterey, my dear Watson.

WATSON

> Very good, Holmes.

SCENE 22

THE HOTEL LOBBY. WHERE ELSE?

As carefully as a mother with her child, Watson guides the famous Ironside, wheelchair and all. . .

> This way, Commissioner Ironside

. . .into the death room, flicking a hand grenade into the chariot's glove compartment. Too late he warns. . .

> Behind you!

. . .and closes the door.

SCENE 23

HOTEL – THE UPSTAIRS ROOM.

WATSON

> Four down. "Burglar's entrance?" Five and five.

SCENE 24

THE HOTEL LOBBY. NUFF SAID?

WATSON

Ah! Mr. James Bond?

"M"

No.

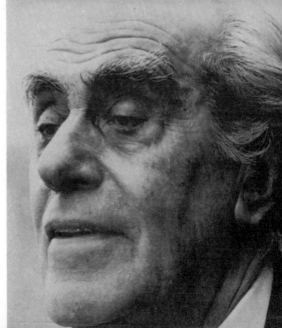

WATSON

You mean not *any* of them?

"M"

No, I'm "M". I felt it was time I had some ACTION!

Cue enough for the redoubtable Doctor who, opening the death room door for the last but one time, checks his quarry's credentials. . .

WATSON

Are you licensed to be killed?

"M"

Er. . .I don't think they mentioned. . .

WATSON

We'll have to risk it then. ACTION!

SCENE 25

HOTEL – THE UPSTAIRS ROOM.

WATSON

That's twenty-five down. One to go. "Cowardly fish with a sting in its tail."

HOLMES

Yellow mantaray, my dear Watson!!

WATSON

Brilliant Holmes. That's the lot I think. I'll just pop down and see if they're all ready.

"Yellow mantaray, my dear Watson!!

SCENE 26

THE HOTEL LOBBY.

As Watson peruses the list of guests, McCloud, the Texan Cowboy appears through the hotel entrance on horseback.

WATSON

And you're. . .?

McCLOUD

McCloud's the name. Dr. Watson, I presume?

WATSON

Correct.

McCLOUD

Where can I park my hoss?

WATSON

This way, please.

McCloud dismounts and the helpful Doctor ties his horse to the Reception Desk, leading the legendary cowboy to his untimely death. There is the sound of a. . .

Thar ya go

. . .followed by the thud of an arrow that has found its home. . . and a moan. . .

INDIANS!

Watson, brushing himself down, with a. . .

Thar you go Mr. McCloud

. . .turns the corner to find ANOTHER Watson. They (the two Watsons) observe each other with astonishment.

REAL WATSON

Good Lord!

FALSE WATSON

Good Lord!!

REAL WATSON

Good Lord!!!

FALSE WATSON

Good Lord!!!!

REAL WATSON

Good Lord!!!!! I'm sorry, but your face seems awfully familiar.

FALSE WATSON

You didn't sit next to me at school did you?

REAL WATSON

I've got it! It's Watson, isn't it?

FALSE WATSON

Watson! That rings a bell!

— peering thoughtfully —

REAL WATSON

Dr. Watson.

— introducing himself, that is —

FALSE WATSON

How do you do, doctor.

— sharply —

Where did you train, St. Thomas's??

REAL WATSON

Yes.

FALSE WATSON

So did I.

REAL WATSON

Ah well, that would be it then.

FALSE WATSON

Well, well, well.

REAL WATSON

Well, well, well . . .

REAL WATSON

— still staring tactfully —

Fancy seeing you here.

Still completely puzzled. . .

What are you doing here, incidentally?

FALSE WATSON

I'm here for the convention.

REAL WATSON

So am I. I work with Arthur Sherlock Holmes.

FALSE WATSON

. . . What an extraordinary thing! So do I!!

REAL WATSON

Good Lord!

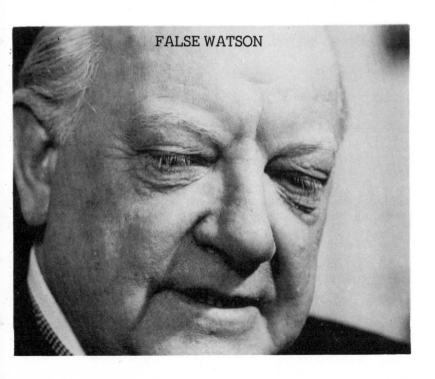

FALSE WATSON

FALSE WATSON

>Good Lord!!

REAL WATSON AND FALSE WATSON

>Good Lord!!!

REAL WATSON

>What a coincidence!

FALSE WATSON

>Amazing!

At this moment Holmes walks round the corner, sees them both and remarks casually:

HOLMES

>Ah hallo, you two. There you are.

He looks away, pauses, and looks back, eyes narrowed.

REAL WATSON AND FALSE WATSON
— in cheerful unison —

>Hallo Holmes!

Holmes looks from one to the other. There is a pause.

FALSE WATSON

>I'm sorry. I believe you know Dr. Watson, don't you?
>Arthur Sherlock-Holmes, Dr. Watson.

HOLMES
— shaking hands thoughtfully —

>How do you do?

REAL WATSON

>Hallo Holmes.

There is a further pause. . .

REAL WATSON
– to Holmes –

>You know Dr. Watson, obviously.

FALSE WATSON

>Eighteen years actually.

REAL WATSON

>Oh! Same as us!

HOLMES

>. . . excuse me a moment.

Holmes walks away and goes into a thinking routine. As he stands by the door of the death room, it slowly swings open, revealing the carnage. Holmes snaps his fingers, and turns to the Watsons.

HOLMES

>Gentlemen. I will come straight to the heart of the matter.
>Prepare yourselves for a shock. Only one of you is Dr. Watson.

FALSE WATSON

>Good Lord!

REAL WATSON

>Good Lord!!

FALSE WATSON

>Good Lor. . .

HOLMES

>Don't start that!

FALSE WATSON

>Sorry, Holmes.

"Gentlemen. . .only one of you is Watson"

HOLMES

Now . . .

REAL WATSON
– *to himself* –

Good Lord!

HOLMES

Stop that!

REAL WATSON

Sorry, Holmes.

HOLMES

. . . it therefore follows, as night follows day, that one of you is masquerading as the other.

FALSE WATSON AND REAL WATSON
– *quickly* –

Good Lord, good Lord, Good Lor . . .

HOLMES

Stop it! Shut up! Will you stop saying "Good Lord".

FALSE WATSON AND REAL WATSON

Sorry, Holmes.

REAL WATSON

Masquerading as the other?

HOLMES

Yes.

FALSE WATSON

You mean he's pretending to me and I'm pretending to be him?

HOLMES

No! No! What would be the point of that?!

FALSE WATSON

I don't know, it's your idea.

HOLMES

No it's not.

REAL WATSON

Well *I* thought you said. . .

HOLMES

Be quiet! Now one of you is Watson. . . but which?

REAL WATSON

We could be twins, Holmes.

HOLMES

What?

REAL WATSON

Supposing we were twins. We'd both be Watson then.

HOLMES
— *to Real Watson* —

Have you got a twin, Watson?

REAL WATSON

No . . . but *he* might have!

HOLMES

Look, if he had a twin it couldn't be you could it.

REAL WATSON

Why not?

HOLMES

Because you'd know.

REAL WATSON

How?

HOLMES

Because you'd be *him!*

REAL WATSON

Good Lord, So I would

HOLMES

Now. . .

REAL WATSON

Your powers of deduction never cease . . .

HOLMES

Shut up!

— walking away from them thoughtfully —

So one of you is an impostor.

FALSE WATSON AND REAL WATSON

Good Lord!

— quickly —

Good Lord, good Lor . . .

HOLMES

Shut up. Will you both shut up saying 'Good Lord', it's
driving me mad!! It's bad enough with one of you.

FALSE WATSON AND REAL WATSON

. . .Sorry, Holmes.

REAL WATSON

Is it me, Holmes?

HOLMES

What?

REAL WATSON

Am I the impostor?

HOLMES

. . . You mean you don't know!!?

REAL WATSON

No.

FALSE WATSON

You're the detective, Holmes.

HOLMES

I haven't worked it out yet!

REAL WATSON

Well how am *I* supposed to know then?

HOLMES

Because if you're the impostor you're imposting and if you're *not* imposting you're *not!!* How can anything be clearer than that.

REAL WATSON
— to False Watson —

Beyond me.

FALSE WATSON

'Fraid so.

REAL WATSON

Leave it to him, he'll sort it out for us.

HOLMES
—turns sharply and, taking piece of paper out of his breast pocket, poses a question —

Your attention please, gentlemen. Why do the Arabs have all the oil and the Irish all the potatoes?

BOTH WATSONS

I don't know, Holmes.

HOLMES

Because the Irish had first pick.

REAL WATSON

Don't Arabs like potatoes, Holmes?

HOLMES

What? No, No. . .it was the Irish who had the first pick.

FALSE WATSON

Oh I see — they used the pick to dig out the potatoes.

HOLMES

No. . .look. . .it was a choice. . .a choice between them.

REAL WATSON

Why was the choice between the Arabs and the Irish? What's happened to good old England?

HOLMES

On this particular occasion. . .stuff good old England. . .No . . .the choice was between the oil and the potatoes.

FALSE WATSON

But if the Irish had chosen both, they could have cooked the potatoes in the oil, Holmes.

REAL WATSON

That's clever. . .I must remember that.

HOLMES

No! No! Now listen!
The Arabs and the Irish had to choose. . .oh forget it. . . forget it!!! It doesn't matter. It's hopeless. Hopeless. Wait! I have an idea. You know the engraved meerschaum the ex-Shah of Persia presented to me?

REAL WATSON

Er . . . in, oh dear . . . er . . . I don't know, Holmes. Sorry.

HOLMES
— *a smile of triumph suffusing his face* —

I deduce then, that you

— *to False Watson* —

are the impostor, and you

— *to Real Watson* —

are the real Watson.

REAL WATSON

Good Lord.

FALSE WATSON

. . . My God, you're clever, Holmes.

HOLMES

From you . . . that's a compliment.

REAL WATSON

But . . . but how did you deduce I was the real Watson, Holmes?

HOLMES

Because you're so sodding dim! So consistently, relentlessly, **almost** magically half-witted.

REAL WATSON

. . . oh, I see! By jove that's clever, Holmes . . . but! If I'm the real Dr. Watson . . .

FALSE WATSON

Hands up please, gentlemen.

Holmes and the Real Watson turn. The FALSE WATSON has produced a revolver, and now the FALSE WATSON speaks with Mrs. Hudson's voice:

MRS. HUDSON (FALSE WATSON)

. . . or I shall be forced to decorate this lobby with your entrails.

WATSON

. . . Mrs. Hudson.

HOLMES

Exactly, Watson

WATSON

You knew all along.

HOLMES

Since 1964.

MRS. HUDSON (FALSE WATSON)

Oh yes? Then tell me, Mr. Clever Dick Smart Aleck I-told-you-so Holmes . . . why did you let me slaughter all of them?

HOLMES

> . . . Nobody likes competition, Mrs. Hudson

Mrs. Hudson's fingers move up to her face removing bit by bit a superb Watson mask, revealing her true self . . .

> And now the moment of reckoning has arrived.

WATSON

> What moment of reckoning, Mrs. Hudson? Why after all these years?

HOLMES

> Because, Watson, Mrs. Hudson is really Francine Moriarty, grandaughter of the infamous Professor. . .Right, Mrs. Hudson?

MRS. HUDSON
— reverting to her natural American accent —

Spot on Holmesie, baby!

Mrs. Hudson now removes her brown wig revealing long blonde hair; then she removes her glasses and eyebrows; then she tears off her cardigan, revealing low cut sweater. She rips off her skirt, revealing black leather mini-skirt. Her gun — which has Francine engraved on it in gold letters — suddenly pops up a little mirror, so that she can apply some scarlet lipstick.

HOLMES

My God, Mrs. Hudson, you're beautiful!

WATSON

Astounding!

FRANCINE

Better than elementary, my dear Watson. And now Adios.

— she eases back the hammer of the revolver, pointing at Watson —

WATSON

You wouldn't, Mrs. Hudson.

FRANCINE

Yes I would Dr. Watson.

WATSON

No you wouldn't.

FRANCINE

Yes I would.

WATSON

No you wouldn't.

Francine shoots him. He falls.

WATSON

. . . She did, Holmes.

HOLMES

Yes she did. Now give me that gun, Mrs. Hudson, before you hurt somebody.

WATSON
— from floor —

She already has, Holmes.

HOLMES

Somebody important, Watson.

WATSON

Oh!

FRANCINE

Get back, Holmes!

Holmes stops.

I've got something to tell you before you die. When my
grandfather lay drowning at the foot of the Reichenbach
Falls. . .

Holmes corrects her pronunciation.

. . .I swore to him that I would never rest until the last trace
of Holmes was wiped from the face of the earth.

HOLMES

I can understand that. . . but why must you destroy civilisation, as we know it, as well?

FRANCINE

It runs in the family. Goodbye, Holmes.

— *she shoots him* —

HOLMES

So it's come to this after all these years?

FRANCINE

You think sustaining that dumb Scottish accent was fun?

— *she shoots him again* —

HOLMES

Thank you, Mrs. Hudson, that will be all.

FRANCINE

Ms. Moriarty to you, limey schlimiel.

— she shoots him again —

HOLMES

Give me that gun.

Francine shoots him four times.

... I said, give me that gun.

Francine shoots him six times.

I'm going to count to three ... One

— Francine shoots him again —

... two

— she shoots him twice more —

... three.

Francine delivers a fusillade lasting eight seconds.

Don't say you haven't been warned.

— he moves forward —

FRANCINE

Godfrey Daniels, Holmes, you're indestructible.

HOLMES

— straightening up —

Not really. You see, Ms. Moriarty, what you don't know is

that before we set off for this conference, I told Watson to
load your pistol with blanks.

— *stunned silence* —

Didn't I, Watson?

WATSON

Yes, Holmes, you did . . .

FRANCINE

My God!

WATSON

But, Holmes? . . .

HOLMES

And so, as you see, the tables are turned.

WATSON
— *louder* —

Holmes!

HOLMES

Quiet, Watson. It is we, The Holmes, who have triumphed over the Moriartys.

WATSON
— *worried* —

I forgot.

HOLMES

The last trace of your evil breed will be extirpated from this planet, and decent people will be able to lie abed at nights, . . . what did you say?

WATSON
— *embarrassed* —

I forgot . . . er . . . to change the bullets.

HOLMES

You forgot?!

WATSON

Well, there was a lot to do, Holmes.

Holmes puts his hand in his jacket, and pulls it out covered in blood.

HOLMES
— *showing Watson* —

Look at that! Look at it!!!

WATSON

Good Lord! Sorry, Holmes.

HOLMES

Sorry? You're sorry?

— to Francine —

He says he's sorry. *He's* sorry. Oh well that's all right then. Nothing to worry about then, have I? You pillock!

— he collapses —

FRANCINE
— triumphantly —

Goodbye, Holmes. And now, if you'll forgive me, I have to destroy civilisation as we know it.

As she leaves the two precious lifebloods ebbing away. . .

WATSON

     I don't quite know how to apologise, Holmes. I . . .

HOLMES
— grabbing Francine's discarded wig —

     Watson! She's forgotten something!

WATSON

     What, Holmes?

HOLMES

     Your bionic bit.

WATSON

     Has she?

HOLMES

— thrusting wig at him —

     Quick.

Watson starts to put it on. . .

WATSON

     I don't think it's the right size, Hol . . .

HOLMES

     No. Smell it, Watson . . . smell it.

Watson smells it and his bionic nose begins to twitch.

HOLMES

     Go get her boy!

Watson curls himself for a huge leap. Then in slow motion he leaps. Up, up and up. His head crashes against the ceiling and he falls slowly, stunned, crashing to the ground. Holmes looks at him, covered in falling plaster and debris.

Brilliant. Spot on, Watson. Oh it'll be nice being dead. I'll be able to get a few things done.

He falls back senseless.

Has Dr. Watson fractured his skull!?
Will Holmes really die!?!? Will Francine
Moriarty escape unharmed and succeed
in her plan to destroy civilisation, as we
know it?

Cast in order of appearance....

DR. GROPINGER	RON MOODY
THE AIR HOSTESS	HOLLY PALANCE
THE BLACK CIA MAN	VAL PRINGLE
BOTH PRESIDENTS OF THE U.S.A.	JOSS ACKLAND
KLEIN OF THE CIA	BILL MITCHELL
THE OTHER CIA MAN	CHRIS MALCOLM
THE AFRICAN DELEGATE	CHRISTOPHER ASANTE
THE ENGLISH DELEGATE	DENHOLM ELLIOTT
THE 1ST AUSTRALIAN	NICK TATE
MISS HOSKINS	JOSEPHINE TEWSON
THE CHINESE DELEGATE	BURT KWOUK
THE CHIEF COMMISSIONER	STRATFORD JOHNS
MRS. HUDSON, AND	
FRANCINE MORIARTY	CONNIE BOOTH
THE BUS CONDUCTOR	DEREK GRIFFITHS
CONSTABLE AT SCOTLAND YARD	BILLY HAMON
THE 2nd AUSTRALIAN	EDMUND PEGGE
THE INTERCOM MAN	ROBERT KINGDOM
THE TEA LADY	MARIA CHARLES
HOTEL COMMISSIONAIRE	DELANEY O'CONNOR
RECEPTIONIST	MOIRA FOOT
HERCULES POIROT	DUDLEY JONES
COLUMBO	LUIE CABALLERO
M	KENNETH BENDA

Continued overleaf

M's GIRLFRIEND .... CHARLOTTE ALEXAND

STEVE McGARRIT .... MAURICE KAUFMANN

SAM SPADE .... MIKE O'MALLEY

CHIEF IRONSIDE .... JOSEPH BRADY

McCLOUD .... PAUL CHAPMAN

And the false Watson was sometimes Norman Atkyns

AND

IRENE HANDL

IS

NOT

ORSON WELLES.

THE END